HISTORY & GEOGR ANTHROPOL

MW01121658

CONTENTS

Author: **Alpha Omega Staff**
Editor: Alan Christopherson, M.S.
Graphic Design: Alpha Omega Staff

Alpha Omega Publications®

804 N. 2nd Ave. E., Rock Rapids, IA 51246-1759
© MCMXCVIII by Alpha Omega Publications, Inc.   All rights reserved.
LIFEPAC is a registered trademark of Alpha Omega Publications, Inc.

ANTHROPOLOGY

"Man is a curious being." This statement can be understood in two ways: (1) Man is inquisitive and seeks to learn, and (2) Man is unique and should be studied. Both ways of understanding the statement apply to anthropology.

Man is inquisitive and seeks to learn. Some interest in man and his ways of life is found in nearly all human societies. For example, **nonliterate** peoples relate stories about the first man and woman. They tell about the origin of fire, the invention of tools, or the beginnings of ways to obtain food. Descriptive accounts about different groups of people have been made through the centuries. The Greek historian, Herodotus, wrote of the Scythians and Egyptians in the fifth century B.C. Explorers, world travelers, missionaries, and soldiers would return to their homes with accounts of all that they saw. Much that they related was distorted. Their accounts tended to be distorted because they saw exotic people and other ways of life through their own cultural **prejudices**. Nevertheless, these early accounts of man provided a starting point for the science of anthropology.

In this LIFEPAC® you will learn about the science of anthropology and how it differs from other social sciences. You will learn what anthropologists do and how they control their prejudices in their work.

Man is unique and should be studied. No other creature is as widely distributed over the face of the earth as man. He has made his home on the frozen crust of the Arctic Ocean, the barren waste of the Sahara Desert, and the dense rain forest surrounding the Amazon River. He has even lived in space. His way of life is as diverse as the places in which he lives. His physical characteristics vary in color, texture, shape, and size. Yet, beneath all of his variety man is very much the same.

In this LIFEPAC® you will learn the ways in which all people are the same. You will learn why individuals and groups will be different from each other. You will learn how races were formed. Finally, you will see the relationship between the way of life of a people and the environment in which they live.

OBJECTIVES

Read these objectives. The objectives tell you what you will be able to do when you have successfully completed this LIFEPAC.

When you have finished this LIFEPAC, you should be able to:

1. Describe the ways the science of anthropology differs from other social sciences.
2. Explain the origin and nature of culture.
3. Tell how anthropologists control their prejudices in their work.
4. List the ways anthropologists gather information.
5. List the ways all people are the same.
6. Explain why people are different from each other.
7. Explain how human races were formed.
8. Describe the relationship between the way of life of a people and their environment.
9. Explain why all cultures are different from each other.
10. Tell the ways all cultures are the same.

Survey the LIFEPAC. Ask yourself some questions about this study. Write your questions here.

_____

_____

_____

_____

_____

_____

_____

_____

_____

_____

I. THE STUDY OF MAN

Many scholars besides anthropologists are concerned with knowing more about man. Of all the social sciences, anthropology has the widest area of interest. Anthropologists study both literate and nonliterate societies, ancient and **contemporary** ways of life, and extinct and modern human forms.

The best way to learn about man is to study him right where he lives. Anthropologists live among the people they study and often do everything the people do. The anthropologist seeks to understand what life is really like for those he studies. He tries to get an insider's point of view. In this section of the LIFEPAC, you will study about studying man. You will learn about the science of anthropology and how anthropologists go about doing their work.

SECTION OBJECTIVES

Review these objectives. When you have completed this section, you should be able to:

1. Describe the ways the science of anthropology differs from other social sciences.
2. Explain the origin and nature of culture.
3. Tell how anthropologists control their prejudices in their work.
4. List the ways anthropologists gather information.

VOCABULARY

Study these words to enhance your learning success in this section.

band (band). A wandering group of a few families.

bias (bī′ us). Favoring one side too much.

comprehensive (kom′ pri hen′ siv). Including much.

contemporary (kun tem' pu rer' ē). Concerning the present time.

divination (div' u nā' shun). Foreseeing the future.

ethics (eth' iks). Rules of right and wrong.

ethnographer (eth nog' ru fur). Anthropologist who describes a culture.

etiquette (et' u ket). Rules for proper behavior.

folklore (fōk' lôr'). Traditional beliefs and legends of a people.

genealogical (jē' nē u loj' u kul). Concerning family descent.

generalization (jen' ur u lu zā' shun). General principle or rule.

haphazard (hap' haz' urd). Not planned.

holistic (hō lis' tik). Concerning the whole of something.

hygiene (hī' jēn). Rules for health.

kin-group (kin' grüp). A group of related families.

monograph (mon' u graf). A scholarly book about a particular subject.

nonliterate (non lit' ur it). Not able to read or write.

prejudice (prej' u dis). Hastily and unfairly formed opinion.

puberty (pyü' bur tē). Physical beginning of manhood and womanhood.

status (stā' tus). Social position or rank.

subdue (sub dü'). Conquer and control.

tempo (tem' pō). Characteristic pace or rhythm.

trauma (trô' mu). An emotional shock.

Note: All vocabulary words in this LIFEPAC appear in **boldface** print the first time they are used. If you are not sure of the meaning when you are reading, study the definitions given.

Pronunciation Key: hat, āge, cãre, fär; let, ēqual, tėrm; it, īce; hot, ōpen, ôrder; oil; out; cup, pùt, rüle; child; long; thin; /ŦH/ for then; /zh/ for measure; /u/ represents /a/ in about, /e/ in taken, /i/ in pencil, /o/ in lemon, and /u/ in circus.

THE BASIS OF ANTHROPOLOGY

The word *anthropology* is composed of the Greek stem *anthropo-* (man) and the noun ending *-logy* (science). As a word, the literal meaning of *anthropology* is *the science of man*. Anthropologists are scientists who study man and all his activities—his "way of life."

Anthropology is divided into three special studies: archaeology, ethnology, and physical anthropology. Archaeologists are anthropologists. They study man's past. They dig in ancient refuse heaps, explore graves and tombs, and unearth buried cities. Anthropologists can understand much about life in the past by studying the discards of peoples, the foods they ate, and the environments in which they lived. Knowledge of the past gives anthropologists a key for understanding some of the ways of modern man.

Ethnologists are anthropologists concerned with the "way of life" of living peoples. Ethnologists study how people are organized into groups; how they make a living; how they view the world; and how

Digging into the past

they choose their mates, marry, and raise their children. Any group of people can be studied, but ethnologists have concentrated primarily on so-called "primitive" groups. Anthropological studies focused on these groups when it became evident they were dying out. Since the early 1900s ethnologists have been recording passing ways of life in writings, pictures, films, and collections of native goods. Because of their studies, ethnologists have concluded that these groups are not at all primitive. Anthropologists now refer to such peoples as **"nonliterate."**

The third special area of concern is physical anthropology. Physical anthropologists study the similarities and differences among the physical forms of people. Like the archaeologists they examine ancient or fossil forms of people. Like the ethnologists they examine modern or living forms. A primary purpose of this area of anthropology is to understand the genetic basis for the physical differences among living peoples. The differences between ancient or fossilized human forms and modern human forms are also studied.

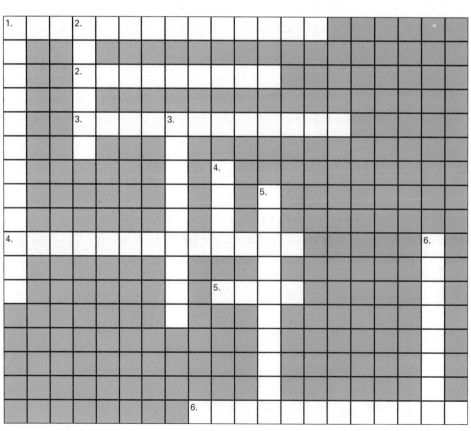

Complete the vocabulary crossword.

1.1

ACROSS
1. General principle or rule.
2. Not planned.
3. Concerning the present time.
4. Including much.
5. A wandering group of a few families.
6. Anthropologist who describes a culture.

DOWN
1. Concerning family descent.
2. Rules of right and wrong.
3. Rules for proper behavior.
4. Favoring one side too much.
5. Foreseeing the future.
6. Traditional beliefs and legends of a people.

 Complete these statements.

1.2   The literal meaning of *anthropology* is _____ .

1.3   Anthropologists who study the ways of living peoples are called

_____ .

1.4   Archaeologists are interested in man's _____ .

1.5   Anthropologists who study human forms are called

_____ .

1.6   Anthropologists who learn about the past by studying the buried discards of a civilization are called _____ .

 **Match these vocabulary words with their definitions.**

1.7	_____ holistic	a. hastily and unfairly formed opinion
1.8	_____ hygiene	b. an emotional shock
1.9	_____ kin-group	c. concerning the whole of something
1.10	_____ monograph	d. characteristic pace or rhythm
1.11	_____ nonliterate	e. rules for health
1.12	_____ prejudice	f. conquer and control
1.13	_____ puberty	g. group of related families
1.14	_____ status	h. social position or rank
1.15	_____ subdue	i. scholarly book about a particular subject
1.16	_____ tempo	j. physical beginning of manhood and womanhood
1.17	_____ trauma	k. not able to read or write

Answer this question.

1.18   What two kinds of human forms do physical anthropologists study?

a. _____   b. _____

Answer this question.

1.19   Why have ethnologists focused their study on "nonliterate" peoples?

_____

_____

Although anthropologists study every aspect of mankind, anthropology is not the only science concerned with humans. Anatomy, physiology, embryology, and genetics are sciences of the physical structures and processes of living things, including man. Biology and zoology are sciences through which the similarities and differences between humans and all forms of animal life are examined. Human behavior is studied in the sciences of psychology, sociology, and history. The ways man relates to his fellows comprises the subject matter of political science. The ways man makes his living is studied in economics. Man's methods of relating to the supernatural is the focus of religious studies. Ecology is the study of the relationship of man and his environment. Human language is the focus of study in linguistics. Like anthropology, all of these sciences focus on man to learn about his physical form and social behavior. Anthropologists take the information these other sciences discover and use it to help them in their own research. Much overlap occurs between anthropology and other sciences concerned with man. Nevertheless, anthropology differs from all of the other human sciences in its central problem, its goal, and its method of analysis.

The central problem of anthropology. Man is unique among all of God's creation. Before He formed man from the dust and woman from man, God determined to make humans different from all

other creatures. God said in Genesis 1:26 that man was to "...have dominion over the fish of the sea, and over the fowl of the air, and over the cattle, and over all the earth, and over every creeping thing that creepeth upon the earth." Man was equipped and told in Genesis 1:28 to "... Be fruitful, and multiply, and replenish the earth, and subdue it..."

The way in which man **subdues** his environment is known to anthropologists as *culture*. Culture includes the way food is obtained, prepared, and eaten; the material, style, and method of construction of a shelter; and the way people communicate, visit, marry, raise children, trade, and travel. Culture is any information or behavior that is learned, shared by society, and passed on to the next generation. That is, culture is a learned human custom. The study of culture is the primary difference between anthropology and the other social sciences.

1.20   The ability of man to have culture comes from _____ .
    a. man   c. God
    b. the environment   d. the opera

1.21   Culture is the way man _____ his environment.
    a. submits   c. submerges
    b. subdues   d. substitutes

1.22   The science concerned with culture is _____ .
    a. anatomy   c. genetics
    b. ecology   d. anthropology

1.23   Culture is only found among _____ .
    a. Americans   c. "primitives"
    b. animals   d. man

The goal of anthropology. Thousands of groups of people live on the earth. Some groups are large (nations) and others are small (**bands**). Each group has its own characteristic style of life, or culture. The goal of anthropology is to discover the regularities in human custom that exist among these groups. Knowing the regularities, anthropologists can make **generalizations** about human behavior.

At the beginning of this century, Arnold van Gennep noted that birth, **puberty**, marriage, and death are accompanied by ceremonies in all groups. Although the details of the ceremonies differ from one group to another, the significance is constant. The social marking of a person passing from one stage in life to the next is considered to be cultural regularity. Anthropologists call such ceremonies "rites of passage."

In addition to rites of passage, anthropologists have found many other elements common to all social groups. These widespread elements are known as cultural "universals." Cultural universals include the following items:

athletic sport	joking
bodily adornment	**kin-groups**
calendar	language
community organization	law
cooking	magic
cooperative labor	meal times
courtship	medicine
dancing	mourning
decorative art	music
divination	numerals
education	personal names
ethics	property rights
etiquette	religious rituals
family	social concepts
feasting	**status**
folklore	differentiation
games	surgery
gestures	tool making
gift giving	trade
greetings	visiting
housing	weather control
hygiene	

These and other elements provide the basic material for anthropological analysis. The main concern in the study of cultural universals would be to explain why people who are so scattered from one another do the same kinds of things. For example, why do all societies have cooperative labor, kin-groups, and language? Are these behaviors inherited or learned? Where did they originate? Why do they appear in isolated groups? In addition, anthropologists want to explain the differences among the details of these universals. For example, why does housing style, size, and material differ among groups? Why all people do not get their food in the same way? The goal of anthropology is to answer questions such as these.

Answer these questions.

1.24   What is the goal of anthropology?_____

_____

1.25   What cultural regularity did Arnold van Gennep discover?_____

_____

Complete these activities. Circle the correct answer.

1.26   Choose the correct rite of passage for the following ceremony:
baby shower
a. birth   b. puberty
c. marriage   d. death

1.27   Choose the correct rite of passage for the following ceremony:
graduation
a. birth   b. puberty
c. marriage   d. death

1.28   Choose the correct rite of passage for the following ceremony:
wedding
a. birth   b. puberty
c. marriage   d. death

1.29   Choose the correct rite of passage for the following ceremony:
funeral
a. birth   b. puberty
c. marriage   d. death

1.30   Choose the correct rite of passage for the following ceremony:
infant baptism
a. birth   b. puberty
c. marriage   d. death

1.31   Choose the correct rite of passage for the following ceremony:
Sweet Sixteen party
a. birth   b. puberty
c. marriage   d. death

1.32   Choose the correct rite of passage for the following ceremony:
wake
a. birth   b. puberty
c. marriage   d. death

1.33   Choose the correct rite of passage for the following ceremony:
honeymoon
a. birth   b. puberty
c. marriage   d. death

1.34   List five cultural universals.
a. _____

b. _____

c. _____

d. _____

e. _____

8

The method of analysis in anthropology. Anthropologists use the comparative method to study man in his cultural variety. The comparative method is the procedure of comparing cultural similarities as well as differences among various societies. This procedure helps anthropologists find regularities in culture. The comparative method also gives an anthropologist a worldwide background for understanding any part of a society's culture. That is, the information anthropologists have gotten by studying many societies will enable them to understand something about one society.

Anthropology is **holistic** in obtaining cultural information used for comparison. It is not limited to the study of religion, warfare, or any other single part of a society's culture. The anthropologist tries to understand every aspect of a particular culture.

Anthropology is both historically and geographically **comprehensive**. Both simple and complex societies are examined. Ancient societies yield cultural information about themselves from the literature of their period and from their material remains. Information about present societies is compiled from many sources such as world travelers, missionaries, soldiers, government officials, and trained **ethnographers**.

The truth of any anthropological conclusions about human behavior depends on the accuracy of the cultural information used. To obtain good cultural data, professional ethnographers are needed. Branislaw Malinowski, a British anthropologist, began training ethnographers at the London School of Economics in 1920. Malinowski stressed that ethnographers needed to live among the people they study for at least two years. During this time an ethnographer was to fully participate in the daily round of activities, learning all he could about the native people.

An ethnographer must ensure that his findings describe the life of a people as it really is. His findings must not be **biased**. When an ethnographer evaluates a culture, he must not allow his own culture to color his conclusions. For example, if the ethnographer eats his food with chopsticks, he should not expect other cultures to do the same or pass judgement on them for being different.

Ethnographers attempt to be "culturally relative," basing evaluations on the native person's point of view. They attempt to avoid two extreme interpretations of a foreign culture: (1) the "noble savage," and (2) ethnocentrism. The noble savage would be someone who is from a nonliterate culture that the ethnographer considers superior to his own. Finding one's own culture superior to another culture has been labeled "ethnocentrism" by those who believe that all cultures are equal.

Sometimes people who make a distinction based on moral standards are accused of being ethnocentric—considering their own culture superior to others. Christians recognize, however, that all human cultures reflect man's sinful nature and should be evaluated according to God's truth, not man's opinion. Missionaries are taught to distinguish between issues that are merely relating to custom and issues relating to God's Word.

 Complete these activities.

1.35 Define the comparative method in anthropology.

_____

_____

1.36   The comparative method helps anthropologists to find _____ in culture and gives a _____ background for understanding any part of a society's _____ .

1.37   Which of the following are methods used to help an anthropologist control his bias? (Place a check mark next to the correct answers.)

_____ evaluate culture from native person's point of view.

_____ use his own culture to color his conclusions.

_____ live among the people and participate in their culture.

Match these items.

1.38 _____ began training ethnographers

1.39 _____ study every aspect of culture

1.40 _____ evaluating from native's point of view

1.41 _____ comparing things among various societies

1.42 _____ seeing foreign culture as inferior to own

1.43 _____ seeing foreign culture as superior to own

a. comparative method

b. noble savage

c. missionaries

d. Branislaw Malinowski

e. ethnocentrism

f. holistic

g. culturally relative

h. Arnold van Gennep

THE SCIENCE OF ANTHROPOLOGY

The science of anthropology is rooted in fieldwork. In fieldwork, people are studied where they live. Any person is able to record what he sees in a foreign society. However, just writing down what one sees is not necessarily useful to the science of anthropology. A person must obtain proper tools and training to be an anthropologist. He must develop certain skills and attitudes that will enable him to work successfully among a foreign people. He also must possess abilities in communication to be able to share with others what he has learned.

Preparing for fieldwork. Studying anthropology courses is most important in preparing for fieldwork. Anthropology courses in colleges and universities are usually taught by trained and experienced anthropologists. These teachers bring to the classroom firsthand information about fieldwork.

Anthropology is not a **haphazard** science. Its goal is to discover regularities in culture. Distinct social groups are like laboratories used for discovering and verifying specific cultural truths. An ethnographer goes to the field with a certain problem he would like to test. For example, he might like to know if leadership in a farming community is related to the size of a person's crop. An ethnographer does not study a society to learn everything in general and nothing in particular about that society.

Once an anthropologist has a problem in mind, he selects the best society to test the problem. He then reads all he can about the people among whom he will live. If possible, he will learn the language spoken there before going to the field.

In addition to the material needed for survival, the field worker takes recording equipment with him. He usually takes cameras, a computer, a tape recorder, pencils, and plenty of paper.

The ethnographer is expected to study the society "in the field" a minimum of one year. This time limit will allow him to observe all of the seasonal activities in the annual cycle of social life. Preparations for the physical and emotional needs of the field worker are very important. Medical, health, and hygiene supplies must be purchased. Proper clothing for the climate must be obtained. Enough money must be secured to pay the costs of equipment, travel, and native helpers. The field worker also must be emotionally prepared to endure loneliness. He will be a social and cultural oddity in a society of strangers. The immediate **trauma** of adjusting to a whole new way of life is known as *culture shock*. This shock may affect both the physical and the emotional process of the ethnographer and could last for weeks. All these needs must be met or fieldwork could be defeating to an ethnographer. However, these promises of support from the Word of God give assurance to the Christian ethnographer:

Philippians 4:19: "...God shall supply all your need according to his riches in glory by Christ Jesus."

Hebrews 13:5: "...[God] hath said, I will never leave thee, nor forsake thee."

▶ ▶ ▶ **Write** *true* **or** *false* **in the blank.**

1.44 _____ Anthropology courses are not important for doing fieldwork.

1.45 _____ Human groups are like laboratories for an anthropologist.

1.46 _____ An anthropologist knows nothing about a group of people before he goes to live among them.

1.47 _____ The only preparation necessary for fieldwork is to obtain equipment and supplies.

1.48 _____ Anthropologists often have difficulty adjusting to a new way of life.

Doing the fieldwork. The principal task of the field worker is to gather information that will allow him to confidently resolve the problem he wanted to test. The information he needs lies in the behavior of individuals as they go about their daily round of activities. However, an ethnographer cannot observe everyone doing everything at all times. The information he uses must be selected from what is going on all around him.

The basic way an ethnographer learns about a society's culture is by living according to that society's standards. He learns the rules for proper behavior and participates in the daily life of the people. The method of studying a way of life by living that life is called *participant observation*.

Ethnographers use "insiders" to collect data on the culture. Certain individuals can greatly help the ethnologist understand a culture from an insider's point of view. The people who are highly knowledgeable and willing to talk about their culture are called *key informants*. Old people are usually a good source of information because they can describe life in the past and compare it to the present. They also have time to sit and talk. People such as healers, priests, and chiefs possess information that is not known to the whole group. They can give important cultural information to the ethnographer.

Understanding culture from the inside

An ethnographer can learn much about a culture by understanding what individuals think about themselves and their way of life. Psychological tests can be given to determine how an individual feels about his physical and cultural surroundings. A person who tells his life history will reveal his inner feelings and will also help the ethnographer to understand the past. Knowing the past helps the field worker understand the present.

All people behave toward each other according to their individual positions in society. That is, all societies have social organization. Examples of social organization include kinship relationships, age relationships, and community political relationships. An ethnographer must know the kinds of relationships that exist between individuals. Only then can he understand the behavior between persons.

The kinship relationships in the society can be discovered by using the **genealogical** method of investigation. In this method the ethnographer asks for the names of a person's relatives and how that person refers to them.

For example, a Crow Indian refers to his mother as "mother" and to his mother's sister as "mother." Although he knows which woman gave him birth, he will behave toward these two women in the same way. They are his "mothers." When the ethnographer knows the kinship relationships between individuals, he will know how each person should act toward one another. He records the genealogical relationships on a kinship chart.

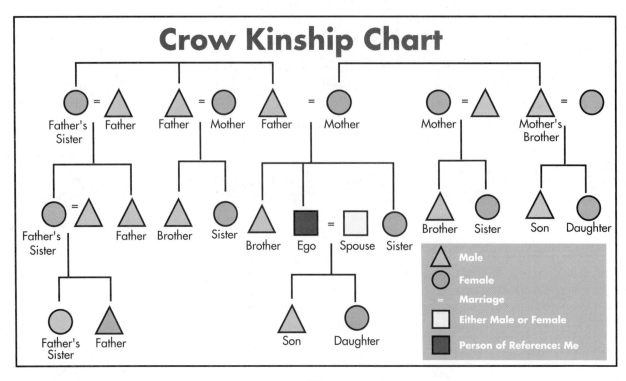

Crow Kinship Chart

The ethnographer also can take a census to learn more about a group's social organization. A census will be used to record marriages, births, deaths, family size, occupations, economic holdings, and so forth. Maps can be drawn to record the location of dwellings, fields, water sources, trade centers, religious centers, and the surrounding territories. One of the best tools an anthropologist can use to understand another culture is the language of that culture. The language reveals how that culture relates to the world. For example, English has dozens of names for colors, but the language of the Hanunóo of the Philippines has only four basic color names. However, unlike English, Hanunóo color names are associated with the qualities of wetness, dryness, lightness, and darkness. These additional qualities of color could be useful for distinguishing an edible green leaf from a inedible one of similar structure.

The field worker should try to keep a diary of his daily activities, thoughts, and moods. His own moods will affect his observations of those people and activities around him. The record of his personal life will help him to evaluate the objectivity of his field report.

Objectivity and accuracy are essential to good fieldwork. To help provide objectivity and accuracy the ethnographer should use cameras and tape recorders. These tools are useful for recording the events that actually happened and for sharing those events with others.

Complete these statements.

1.49   The method of studying a culture by doing what the people of that culture do is called _____ .

1.50   Knowledgeable individuals who tell the ethnographer much about their culture are known as_____ .

1.51   The ethnographer learns how people feel about themselves through
a. _____ tests and by asking them about their
b. _____ history.

1.52   The _____ method is a way to learn the kinship relationships in a society.

1.53   A record of events like marriages, births, deaths, and occupations is called a _____ .

Match these items.

1.54   _____ language

1.55   _____ diary

1.56   _____ camera and tape recording

a. provides objective and accurate information

b. reveals how the culture relates to the world

c. shows how field worker's mood is affected by observation

Presenting the fieldwork. After returning from the field, the ethnographer begins to sort out all of his material and data. He tries to make sense out of his field notes, interviews, tests, genealogies, censuses, and maps. He must generalize into one view all of the realities of the cultural world he experienced. After this process, the writing of his findings will begin.

The standard form for presenting the findings of fieldwork is the ethnographic **monograph**. The *general* ethnographic monograph usually is organized under subject headings such as these: location and physical environment, kinship and social organization, law and social control, economics and technology, religion, politics, art, and social change and continuity. The general monograph treats each of these topics equally, giving a holistic view of the culture of the society. However, the general monograph can be misleading because of its organization. When a culture description is divided into separate subject areas, the culture itself might be thought to exist in a separated form. In reality, a culture is all of one piece, not a collection of separate pieces. Many ethnographers now write *specialized* ethnographic monographs. These works focus on one part of a culture: religion, economics, kinship, polit-ical processes, and so forth. The specialized monograph usually will show the relationships between one specific aspect of a culture and every other aspect.

Another form for presenting the fieldwork is the life history account of one member of the culture. The life history form is valuable because it gives the insider's view of the culture. However, it is not the best method to use to present a complete view of a culture. The life history account is subject to distortions and bias because it is the view of only one person. The informant might not have been completely accurate in remembering and relating his life history to the ethnographer.

The ethnographic film has great value for accuracy and impact. A film allows one to visualize the people as they live out a scene from a real-life drama. Movement, space, shape, and **tempo** are part of a culture. They can be understood best when they are seen. Films provide a historical record. They portray what life was like at some specific time in the past. Films also allow a cultural event of the past to be compared with the same event of the present. This comparison will reveal the nature of the cultural changes that have occurred since the film was made.

Write the letter of the best answer in the blank. Answers may be used more than once.

1.57 _____ presents an insider's view of the culture

1.58 _____ gives a holistic view of the culture

1.59 _____ presents movement, space, shape, and tempo of a culture

1.60 _____ could make culture appear to be separated

1.61 _____ the view of only one person

1.62 _____ focuses on one aspect of culture

1.63 _____ useful for historical comparison

1.64 _____ presents relationships between aspects of a culture

a. general ethnographic monograph

b. specialized ethnographic monograph

c. life history account

d. ethnographic film

Review the material in this section in preparation for the Self Test. The Self Test will check your mastery of this particular section. The items missed on this Self Test will indicate specific areas where restudy is needed for mastery.

SELF TEST 1

Match these items (each answer, 2 points).

1.01 _____ physical anthropologist

1.02 _____ Arnold van Gennep

1.03 _____ life history

1.04 _____ census

1.05 _____ archaeologist

1.06 _____ key informant

1.07 _____ general monograph

1.08 _____ psychological tests

1.09 _____ ethnologist

1.010 _____ specialized monograph

1.011 _____ ethnographic film

1.012 _____ trash heaps

1.013 _____ Branislaw Malinowski

1.014 _____ diary

1.015 _____ kinship chart

a. presents all aspects of a culture

b. show relationships among people

c. studies human forms

d. helps an ethnographer understand himself

e. noted life-crisis ceremonies

f. began training ethnographers

g. one person's view of his culture

h. reveals life in the past

i. list of marriages, births, deaths, and so on

j. provides a visual record

k. digs up ancient ruins

l. focuses on one aspect of culture

m. gives ethnographer much information

n. studies culture of living peoples

o. reveals inner feelings

Write the correct letter in the blank (each answer, 2 points).

1.016 Rites of passage, joking, music, and family are cultural _____ .
a. ceremonies   b. universals   c. problems   d. biases

1.017 The study of all aspects of culture makes anthropology _____ .
a. thorough   b. comparative   c. a science   d. holistic

1.018 The goal of anthropology is to discover cultural _____ .
a. shocks   b. people   c. regularities   d. prejudices

1.019 Anthropology differs from other human sciences through its emphasis on

_____ .

a. culture   b. primitives   c. nonliterates   d. man

1.020   Anthropologists should stay in the field at least one year to see _____.
         a. all the people   c. a key informant
         b. all seasonal activities   d. rites of passage

1.021   Cultural originally comes from _____.
         a. man   b. God   c. Noah   d. Babel

1.022   Anthropology tries to understand every aspect of a culture because anthropology is _____.
         a. comparative   b. relative   c. biased   d. holistic

1.023   Anthropology focuses on "nonliterate" societies because _____.
         a. they are dying out   c. they are older
         b. they are more diverse   d. they are easier to analyze

Put these events in the proper order: first, second, third, and so on (each answer, 2 points).

1.024   _____   Read about the people.

1.025   _____   Choose a society to test the problem.

1.026   _____   Leave the field.

1.027   _____   Adjust to the new culture.

1.028   _____   Study anthropology courses.

1.029   _____   Enter the field.

1.030   _____   Write about the culture.

1.031   _____   Observe and record cultural events.

1.032   _____   Formulate a problem to test.

1.033   _____   Sort out the cultural information.

Complete these statements (each answer, 3 points).

1.034   The ethnographer would be wise to learn a people's _____
         because this is the way people perceive and relate to their world.

1.035   The method for discovering cultural similarities and differences is

         _____ .

1.036   Two extreme interpretations of a foreign culture are known as
         a. _____ and b. _____ .

1.037   Two tools for discovering the social organization of a group are a.
         _____ and b. _____ .

1.038   Difficulty in adjusting to a new way of life is called _____ .

1.039   Studying a way of life by living that life is called _____
         observation.

16

Put a check next to the answers that are correct (each answer, 2 points).

1.040　Which of the following are cultural universals?

____ fairy tales	____ property rights
____ greetings	____ ethics
____ feasting	____ polytheism
____ child marriage	____ agnostic philosophy
____ law	____ family

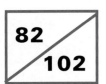

82 / 102

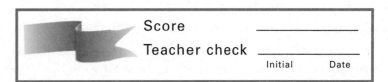

Score _____

Teacher check _____

Initial　　　Date

II. THE NATURE OF MAN

Man is the most numerous of all the giant forms of life. He is considered large when all of the creatures on earth are compared for size. Obviously, whales, elephants, and hippopotamuses are larger than man, but very few creatures attain their dimensions. Most living things are much smaller than man. Some are so small they can be seen only through a microscope.

Mankind is different from all other forms of life. He is the only being who walks upright, manufactures the things he needs to help him in life, writes, and worships God. Differences also exist between the many groups of people scattered over the earth. They differ in skin color, hair color and texture, language characteristics, daily activities, and many other ways. Yet, as *man*, people are very much the same. In this section of the LIFEPAC, you will study the nature of man, what he is like as a physical being. You will learn about the ways all people are alike and how certain physical differences came about.

SECTION OBJECTIVES

Review these objectives. When you have completed this section, you should be able to:

5.　List the ways all people are the same.
6.　Explain why people are different from each other.
7.　Explain how human races were formed.

VOCABULARY

Study these words to enhance your learning success in this section.

allele (u lēl'). One of a gene pair.

bipedal (bī' ped ul). Having two feet.

confound (kon found'). Confuse.

coordination (kō ôr' du nā' shun). Working well together.

extremities (ek strem' u tes). External members away from the trunk.

gene pool (jēn' pül). The group within which most marriages take place.

genus (jē' nus). A group of similar things.

heterozygous (het' ur u zī' gus). Having different alleles for one gene.

homozygous (hō' mu zī' gus). Having identical alleles for one gene.

intramarriage (in' tru mar' ij). Marriages within the same group.

manipulate (mu nip' yu lāt). To handle skillfully.

potential (pu ten' shul). Capable of coming into being.

taxa (tak' su). Arrangements in groups.

THE UNITY OF MAN

All people wear a cultural skin. That is, they cover themselves with specific styles of clothing, decorations, and colors. The cultural skin makes one group of people appear to be different from all other groups, but beneath that covering people are very much alike.

People have a common origin. All are composed of the same material and share a common structure and image. No human group is without a language. Every person shares a common inheritance. All humans are members of the same family—man.

People have a common origin.

Common origin. The source of all creation is God. After God had created the earth and made the plants and animals, He created man (Genesis 1:27):

> So God created man in his own image, in the image of God created he him; male and female created he them.

After creating the first man and woman, God gave them the responsibility for producing more people. On the day they were created, God said to them in Genesis 1:28: "...Be fruitful, and multiply, and replenish the earth..." All people who have ever lived have come from Adam and Eve. Adam acknowledged the common origin of all people when he named his wife *Eve* (Genesis 3:20):

> And Adam called his wife's name Eve; because she was the mother of all living.

Common substance. The body of every person is composed of materials commonly found in the earth. The Bible says (Genesis 2:7) man is made of dust:

> And the Lord God formed man of the dust of the ground.

Because we have all come from Adam who was formed out of dust, our bodies are like his in substance. The material of which

we are made is not easily recognized while we are alive. However, when our bodies die, their real substance is known. In Job 3:20, Job said concerning man, "All go unto one place; all are of the dust, and all turn to dust again."

Common structure. All human beings have similar physical structures. Our bodies have paired **extremities**: two feet, two legs, two hands, two arms, two ears, two eyes, and two nostrils. We are **bipedal**, made to walk and run upright without using hands to move about. Each hand has an opposable thumb and is formed for grasping and **manipulating** objects. Quick **coordination** between our eyes and hands is controlled by our brains. Our internal organs are alike in location and function. We all have an internal skeleton that is composed of 206 bones. Indeed, the only significant structural difference between people is the difference of being male and female.

When God created mankind, He created him as male and female. The difference between a male and a female is not a difference in kind—both are "man." This aspect of the nature of man is taught in Genesis 5:2, where God calls both male and female *man*:

> Male and female created he them; and blessed them, and called their name Adam, in the day when they were created.

The name *Adam* means *man*, or *mankind*.

Common image. According to the Bible (Genesis 1:27), "...God created man in his own image, in the image of God created he him; male and female created he them." Being made in God's image gives man great value in God's world. In Genesis 9:6 God's estimation of man's value is seen:

> Whoso sheddeth man's blood, by man shall his blood be shed: for in the image of God made he man.

The value of man is also seen in his relation to the rest of God's creation. The

Psalmist, David, speaks of man in these words in Psalm 8:4 through 8:

> What is man, that thou art mindful of him? And the son of man, that thou visitest him? For thou hast made him a little lower than the angels, and hast crowned him with glory and honor. Thou madest him to have dominion over the works of thy hands; thou hast put all things under his feet: All sheep and oxen, yea, and the beasts of the field; The fowl of the air, and the fish of the sea, and whatsoever passeth through the paths of the seas.

God, Who created all things, allows those in His image to rule over what He has made.

The Hebrew word for *image* means *shadow* and refers to the likeness of something. A person's shadow on the ground has a likeness to that person, but the shadow is not exactly the same as the person. The image of God in varying degrees is seen in all mankind. Like God, man can be conscious of himself and know himself as a person. He has a sense of moral responsibility—he can know good and evil. He can exercise grace by giving to others some of the things given to him.

Match these items.

2.1 _____ bipedal

2.2 _____ confound

2.3 _____ coordination

2.4 _____ extremities

2.5 _____ intramarriage

2.6 _____ manipulate

2.7 _____ potential

a. external members away from the trunk

b. working well together

c. marriages within the same group

d. confuse

e. to handle skillfully

f. having two feet

g. capable of coming into being

Complete these statements.

2.8 The mother of all people was _____ .

2.9 (Genesis 1:27),"... a. _____ b. _____ man in his own c. _____ , in the image of God created he him; male and female created he them."

2.10 The bodies of all people are composed of common elements described in the Bible as _____ .

2.11 The number of bones in a person's body is _____ .

2.12 In Genesis 5:2, both male and female are called _____ .

HISTORY & GEOGRAPHY

704

LIFEPAC TEST

80/100

Name _____

Date _____

Score _____

HISTORY & GEOGRAPHY 704: LIFEPAC TEST

Match these items (each answer, 2 points).

1. _____ psychological tests   a. physical characteristics

2. _____ Branislaw Malinowski   b. reveals inner feelings

3. _____ census   c. one person's view of his culture

4. _____ heterozygous   d. began training professional ethnologists

5. _____ intramarriage   e. study all aspects of culture

6. _____ ethnographic film   f. shows marriages, births, deaths, and so on

7. _____ homozygous   g. identical alleles in a pair

8. _____ holistic   h. different alleles in a pair

9. _____ life history   i. provides an accurate visual record

10. _____ phenotype   j. marriage within own groups

Write the correct letter in the blank (each answer, 2 points).

11. Culture originated in _____ .

     a. man   c. God
     b. nature   d. Boston

12. Culture is the authority and ability of man to _____ .

     a. make alliances   c. subdue his environment
     b. tell the future   d. have fertile offspring

13. Cultures differ from one another because _____ .

     a. races differ   c. languages differ
     b. anthropologists differ   d. environments differ

14. All cultures are alike in that all seek _____ .

     a. alliances, kin, and support   c. rites of passage
     b. food, protection, and prosperity   d. visions, omens, and oracles

Match these items (each answer, 2 points).

15. _____ fieldwork   a. noted rites of passage

16. _____ kinship chart   b. seeing a group as inferior

17. _____ cultural relativism   c. study people where they live

18. _____ intermarriage   d. helps ethnographer understand himself

19. _____ Arnold van Gennep   e. shows relationships among people

20. _____ anthropology   f. gives ethnologists much information

21. _____ kind/species   g. a way to control bias

22. _____ archaeology   h. ability to produce fertile offspring

23. _____ diary   i. marriage with another group

24. _____ ethnocentrism   j. science of man

Write the correct letter in the blank (each answer, 2 points).

25.   People differ physically from one another because _____ .
   a. their alleles differ   c. their languages differ
   b. their environments differ   d. their images differ

26.   All people are the same because they share a common _____ .
   a. origin, structure, and image
   b. village, kin, and occupation
   c. environment, culture, and language
   d. belief, power, and method

Put these events in the proper order (each answer, 2 points).

27.   _____ Races were formed.

28.   _____ All cooperated in building a city and a tower.

29.   _____ The people separated, migrating to new environments.

30.   _____ Each separate population became homozygous for many genes.

31.   _____ Each new language was a barrier to strangers.

32.   _____ All people spoke a common language.

33.   _____ God confused the common language.

Write the correct letter(s) in the blank. Items may have two answers (each answer, 2 points).

34.   _____ migrating food supply   a. hunting and gathering societies

35.   _____ relatively permanent shelters b. horticultural societies

36.   _____ portable or disposable shelters c. fishing societies

37.   _____ wealth, large food reserves   d. pastoral societies

38.   _____ clustered, few shelters

39.   _____ seasonal, social reorganization

Complete these statements (each answer, 3 points).

40.   The goal of anthropology is to discover cultural _____ .

41.   The method of analysis in anthropology is the _____
       method.

42.   The primary way an ethnographer learns about a culture is to live according
       to that society's standards. This is called _____
       _____ .

43.   The standard form of presenting the fieldwork in a holistic way is the general
       ethnographic _____ .

NOTES

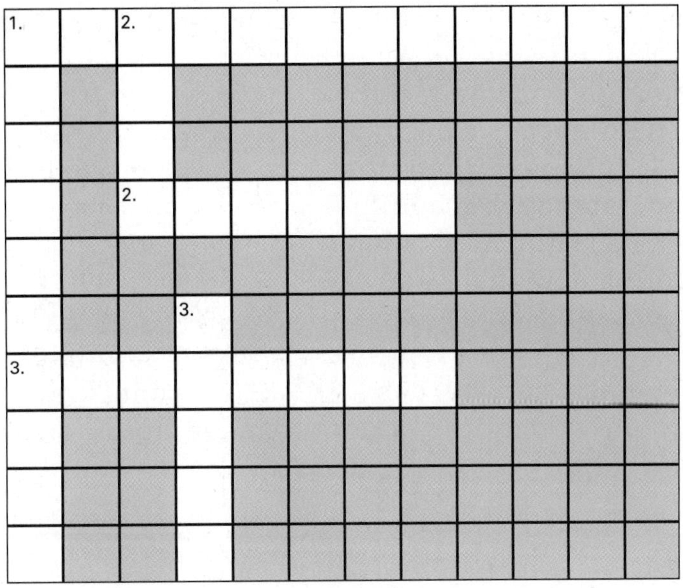

[Crossword grid]

 Complete the crossword.

2.13

ACROSS

1. Having different alleles for one gene.
2. One of a gene pair.
3. The group within which most marriages take place.

DOWN

1. Having identical alleles for one gene.
2. Arrangements in groups.
3. A group of similar things.

Complete these statements.

2.14   Man has value because he was made in the image of _____ .

2.15   Man's value is shown by the fact that God allows him to _____

_____ over creation.

2.16   What does the Hebrew word for *image* mean? _____

2.17   People are like God in that they are a. _____ of themselves

and have a sense of moral b. _____ .

Common language. Many different sounds can be made by the human voice. Those sounds associated with specific meanings within a social group are vocal symbols, or words. An organized set of words expresses a thought. The act of sending and receiving thoughts through word symbols is language. The Bible relates in Genesis 11:1 that at one time "...the whole earth was of one language, and of one speech." When clear communication exists in a society, much work can be done. Without clear communication, a society cannot function effectively. When people had one language and their activities began to displease God, He **confounded** their language. When they could no longer understand one another, they could no longer work together. Man's single society scattered and their activity that displeased God ceased.

A common language does not exist now for the whole world. Each society has its own language, or communication system.

The apostle Paul wrote about the differences in language (1 Corinthians 14:10–11):

> There are, it may be, so many kinds of voices in the world, and none of them is without signification. Therefore if I know not the meaning of the voice, I shall be unto him that speaketh a barbarian (foreigner), and he that speaketh shall be a barbarian unto me.

Every language has meaning for its own society, and every society in the world has a meaningful language.

Write *true* or *false* in the blank.

2.18 _____ Words are sounds that have a specific meaning.

2.19 _____ Mankind has never had a common language.

2.20 _____ Clear communication helps a society stay together.

2.21 _____ Every society has a meaningful language.

Common heritage. All mankind is descended from Adam and partakes of his heritage. The Bible describes Adam's heritage to us in Romans 5:12:

> Wherefore as by one man sin entered into the world and death by sin; and so death passed upon all men, for that all have sinned.

We have inherited sin and death through Adam. An alternative heritage of everlasting life is offered, and this comes only through faith in God's Son, Jesus Christ. The heritage of Adam is inherited; the heritage of Jesus Christ is a gift received. The two heritages available to man are quite clearly presented in John 3:36.

> He that believeth on the Son hath everlasting life: and he that believeth not the Son shall not see life; but the wrath of God abideth on him.

Common kind. Scientists have classified man as belonging to the **genus** *Homo* and the species *sapiens*. Although man today is separated into several races, each race belongs to the species *sapiens*. The Bible does not use the term *species*, but it does teach that all people are of the same "kind." The apostle Paul declared this truth in Acts 17:26:

> [God] hath made of one blood all nations of men for to dwell on all the face of all the earth.

The basis for determining which living things should belong to the same species, or kind, is their ability to have fertile offspring. These offspring are also able to mate and have offspring. This reproductive ability was established by God at Creation. All living things reproduce "after their kind." Because of his ability to reproduce after his kind, man in all of his variety is still man.

2.22   Adam's heritage to us is a. _____ and b. _____ .

2.23   Christ offers us a heritage of _____ life.

2.24   Scientists classify men in the genus _____ and the species _____ .

2.25   The Bible says that man was made "of one _____ ."

2.26   Living things are of the same species when they are able to mate and have _____ offspring.

THE DIVERSITY OF MAN

The physical diversity of man can be seen by even the most casual observer. People differ from each other in both subtle and significant ways. The most noticeable differences among people are:

1. physical height;
2. color of skin, hair, and eyes;
3. texture of hair;
4. shape of eyes, ears, nose, lips, and teeth; and
5. distribution of body hair.

These differences usually sort out into patterns. These patterns allow us to distinguish one type of person from another. No two people look alike. No two people have precisely the same genes, except identical twins. The genetic material a person receives from his parents will influence his physical characteristics, or phenotype.

The definition of race. A race is defined as a human population which can be readily distinguished from any other population based on genetic differences alone. The species *sapiens* can be subdivided into subspecies, or races. Races can also be subdivided into subraces. Modern anthropology separates *sapiens* into six races:

1. Australasid—found around Australia,
2. Europid—found around Europe and the Near East,
3. Negrid—found around central Africa,
4. Khoisanid—found around southwest Africa,
5. Mongolid—found around eastern Asia, and
6. Indianid—found around northern South America.

These classifications are not definitive, and several different types of classifications currently exist.

The Bible distinguishes between peoples and includes **taxa**, arrangements in groups, for human races and subraces in the tenth chapter of Genesis. The last verse of this taxa chapter (Genesis 10:32) states that man is divided into three races through Noah's three sons:

These are the families of the sons of Noah, after their generations, in their nations: and by these were the nations divided in the earth after the flood.

The names commonly associated with the three races are Mongolid (Shem), Negrid (Ham), and Europid (Japheth).

Every race comes from Noah's three sons.

The families of Noah's three sons provided the population that now covers the earth. All of the physical differences among people today have come from the genetic material of Noah's sons and their wives. However, this genetic heritage does not mean that one of Noah's sons was yellow, one was black, and one was white. They probably looked very much the same. Each came from the same parents and received very similar genetic material. Nothing is known about the physical characteristics of their wives.

Father and mother share equally in transmitting to a child their genetic material. Each will contribute one **allele** for every gene in the child. The interaction between a pair of alleles and their interaction with their environment will control the phenotype of the child. For example, if a child inherits one allele for red hair and one for black hair the red will be hidden in his phenotype. His hair will be black. If he inherits alleles for red and light brown hair, his phenotype will be auburn hair. If he inherits alleles for red and blond hair, he will have light red hair.

Alleles act in pairs. If the alleles for a certain gene are identical, the person will be **homozygous** for that gene. Both alleles will be seen in the phenotype of that person. For example, if both alleles from his parents are for black hair, he will have black hair. If the two alleles he receives are different from each other, he will be **heterozygous** for that gene. Only one or the other or a blending of the two alleles will be seen in the phenotype of a heterozygous person. Because a person has thousands of genes, he can be homozygous in some and heterozygous in others. The extremely large numbers of combinations of alleles accounts for the great variety in people's phenotypes.

Match these items.

2.27 _____ Mongolid

2.28 _____ taxa

2.29 _____ *sapiens*

2.30 _____ Ham

2.31 _____ Europid

a. subrace
b. Japheth
c. Negrid
d. Shem
e. Noah
f. Genesis chapter 10
g. species

Answer these questions.

2.32 Why did Noah's three sons probably look the same?_____

_____

_____

2.33 What two factors determine the phenotype of a person?

a. _____

b. _____

2.34 People are different from each other genetically because of the large number of _____ alleles.

The explanation of race. Three elements are necessary for a race to be formed:

1. a population,
2. an environment, and
3. a common language.

After the Flood, the Bible says in Genesis 11:1 that "...the whole earth was of one language, and of one speech." When everyone in a population speaks the same language, the **potential** for cooperation is very great. Fewer barriers exist between

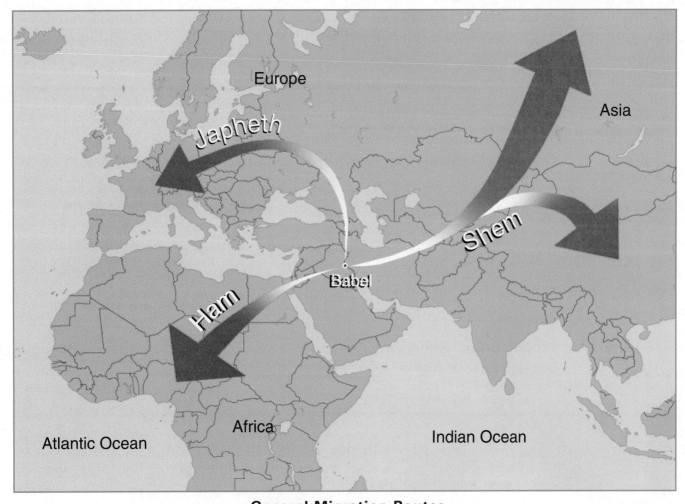

General Migration Routes

people if they can understand each other clearly. The people after the Flood were able to work together smoothly. They were able to accomplish whatever they determined to do. They began to build a city and a tower. Because this activity displeased the Lord, He stopped their building by confusing their language. When men could no longer understand each other, they could not cooperate in a common activity. They scattered from the city called Babel and from each other.

When the Lord confused man's language and scattered the people, they migrated to other parts of the earth in family groups. The general directions of travel followed family ties. The descendants of each one of Noah's three sons separated from those of the other two. Further separation occurred within the three divisions until Noah's descendants were settled in family groups. These groups were sorted into nations according to the new languages they spoke. Each group occupied its own territory in its own nation. As each group of people settled,

they subdued their new environment and developed their own unique culture.

After God confused the original language of man, people could not communicate with anyone outside of their own group. The people of each group had their own new language that enabled them to work together. The new languages were also barriers that separated people. Those who did not know the language of a people were prevented from living among that people.

Because language was a barrier to foreigners, marriages were made between people from the same group. Through generations of **intramarriage**, the genetic material of the people became fairly equally shared within the group. Individuals of the group became homozygous for many of the same kind of genes. The people began to look very much alike. The three separated **gene pools** of Noah's three sons form the basis for the three races of man. Other gene pools separated within a race have produced subraces.

 **Complete these statements.**

2.35 The three elements necessary for a race to be formed are

a. _____,

b. _____, and

c. _____.

2.36 A common _____ enables a community to work together.

2.37 To those who cannot speak the common language, a social _____ exists.

2.38 Groups of individuals become homozygous in genetic structure through generations of _____.

Review the material in this section in preparation for the Self Test. This Self Test will check your mastery of this particular section as well as your knowledge of all previous sections.

SELF TEST 2

Match these items (each answer, 2 points).

2.01	_____ kind	a.	seeing a group as inferior
2.02	_____ phenotype	b.	forms a barrier
2.03	_____ shadow	c.	species
2.04	_____ culture	d.	identical alleles
2.05	_____ Eve	e.	physical appearance
2.06	_____ Adam	f.	studies all aspects of culture
2.07	_____ heterozygous	g.	image
2.08	_____ ethnocentrism	h.	Adam's heritage
2.09	_____ fieldwork	i.	subduing the environment
2.010	_____ alleles	j.	a way to control bias
2.011	_____ cultural relativism	k.	the mother of all living
2.012	_____ sin and death	l.	act in pairs
2.013	_____ holistic	m.	male and female
2.014	_____ homozygous	n.	studying people where they live
2.015	_____ language	o.	different alleles

Complete these statements (each answer, 3 points).

2.016　Anthropologists use the _____ method to analyze cultural similarities and differences.

2.017　The names of the races commonly associated with Noah's three sons are a. _____ , b. _____ , and c. _____ .

2.018　In Biblical terminology, the substance of our bodies is _____ .

2.019　Studying a way of life by living as the people do is called _____ _____ .

2.020　The elements necessary for a race to be formed are a. _____ , an b. _____ , and a common c. _____ .

2.021　Our heritage through Jesus Christ is _____ life.

2.022　Man is like God in that he is a. _____ of himself and has a sense of moral b. _____ .

2.023　List three of the "rites of passage" Arnold van Gennep found that all societies celebrate.

　　　a. _____

　　　b. _____

　　　c. _____

2.024　Man has value because he is made in the image of _____

Put these events in the proper order: first, second, third, and so on (each answer, 2 points).

2.025 _____ Populations became homozygous for some genes.

2.026 _____ The language was a barrier to strangers.

2.027 _____ All people spoke one language.

2.028 _____ Races emerged.

2.029 _____ God confused the language.

2.030 _____ All cooperated in building a city and a tower.

2.031 _____ The people migrated to new environments.

Write the correct letter in the blank (each answer, 2 points).

2.032 The goal of anthropology is to discover regularities in _____ .
a. nature   b. culture   c. genetics   d. observation

2.033 Treating all aspects of culture equally makes anthropology _____ .
a. relative   b. specialized   c. holistic   d. common

2.034 Which of the following is a way men are the same? _____
a. height   b. species   c. language   d. race

2.035 Which discipline studies the physical forms of people? _____
a. physical anthropologists   c. ethnologists
b. zoologists   d. archaeologists

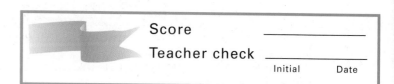

Score _____

Teacher check _____
Initial   Date

III. THE CULTURE OF MAN

Every human group has a culture—they all "subdue" their environments. The type of environment experienced by a social group is reflected in the characteristics of their culture.

Since environmental conditions vary from place to place, the associated cultures will also vary. However, because of the unity and commonality of man, a basic similarity exists among human groups wherever they are settled. All peoples attempt to obtain food, protection, and prosperity for themselves. The manner in which man pursues these goals is influenced greatly by his environment and culture. In this final section of the LIFEPAC, you will study some of the methods people have developed for **sustaining** life in their particular environments. You will learn about the relationship between environment and culture.

SECTION OBJECTIVES

Review these objectives. When you have completed this section, you should be able to:

8. Describe the relationship between the way of life of a people and their environment.
9. Explain why all cultures are different from each other.
10. Tell the ways all cultures are the same.

VOCABULARY

Study these words to enhance your learning success in this section.

alkaloid (al' ku loid). A chemical derived from plants.

alliance (u lī' uns). A joining formed by mutual agreement.

clan (klan). Families that claim descent from a common ancestor.

deplete (di plēt'). Exhaust by using up resources.

durable (dür' u bul). Able to withstand wear, decay.

inherent (in hir' unt). A permanent and essential quality or attribute.

intermarriage (in' tur mar' ij). Marriage between members of different groups.

lean-to (lēn' tu'). A shelter open on one side.

lifestyle (līf' stīl'). Characteristic manner of living.

mutual (myü' chü ul). Each to the other.

nutriment (nü' tru munt). Required for life and growth; nourishment.

obligation (ob' lu gā shun). Duty on account of kinship relation.

subsist (sub sist'). Keep alive; live.

sustain (su stān'). Supply with food and provisions.

terrain (te rān'). Tract of land.

ultimate (ul' tu mit). Coming at the end; final.

watershed (wô' ter shed'). Region drained by a river system.

wicker (wik' ur). A slender, easily bent branch or twig.

SEEKING FOOD

Man needs food to live. He gets his food from plants and animals. The number of people that can live in an area and the general characteristics of the people's culture is determined by their food supply. The number and type of plants and animals in an area also depends on the food available to them. The soil and climate of the area determine the food supply for plants and animals. Because of this food chain, the size and cultural characteristics of a group of people **ultimately** depends on the soil and climate of their area.

In anthropological studies labels are given to types of cultures. People of small, nonliterate societies are labeled according to the way they obtain food.

Generally, people who live in very similar environments throughout the world will be given the same anthropological label.

Hunters and gatherers. A well-studied example of a hunting and gathering people is the Arunta of Central Australia. They number about two thousand and occupy around forty thousand square miles of semidesert **terrain**. Rain is rare and irregular. Vegetation is limited to a few wiry shrubs, coarse tufts of grass, and few acacia trees. The animals living in the area are small and widely scattered. The main method of hunting is the use of a spear made from a sharpened stick. The Arunta **subsist** primarily on kangaroos, birds, snakes, lizards, frogs, snails, caterpillars, grubs, ants, and roots. After one or two days in the same area, the food supply will be used up. The small group will have to move its camp to a new area to find food.

During the irregular rainy season, plants spring to life. Animals become more numerous because of increased vegetation. At this time, the Arunta wander in "bands" composed of two or three families hunting for food. During the dry season, several bands will gather at a water hole frequented by thirsty animals. While assembled in the larger groups, the people engage in social celebrations.

Very little in the Arunta environment is useful for clothing. The few possessions they have are easy to replace. These include wooden spears, bark dishes, digging sticks, and throwing sticks. The simple brush **lean-to** shelters erected are abandoned when the band moves to a new area. Their wandering search for food is difficult. The Arunta carry few possessions.

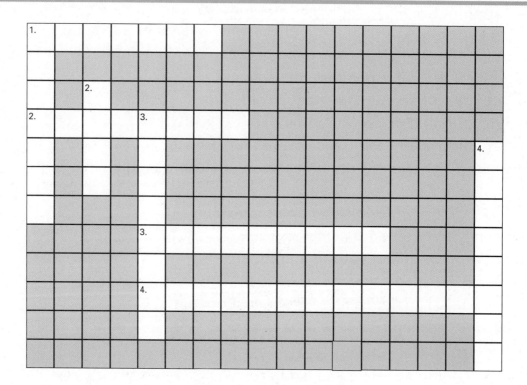

 **Complete the vocabulary crossword.**

3.1   **ACROSS**
  1. Exhaust by using up resources.
  2. A joining formed by mutual agreement.
  3. Characteristic manner of living.
  4. Marriage between members of different groups.
  DOWN
  1. Able to withstand wear, decay.
  2. Families that claim descent from a common ancestor.
  3. A chemical derived from plants.
  4. A permanent and essential quality or attribute.

Match these items.

3.2	_____ lean-to	a. slender, easily bent branch or twig
3.3	_____ mutual	b. shelter open on one side
3.4	_____ nutriment	c. region drained by a river system
3.5	_____ obligation	d. each to the other
3.6	_____ subsist	e. coming at the end; final
3.7	_____ sustain	f. required for life and growth; nourishment
3.8	_____ terrain	g. tract of land
3.9	_____ ultimate	h. duty on account of kinship relation
3.10	_____ watershed	i. supply with food and provisions
3.11	_____ wicker	j. keep alive; live

 Complete these statements.

3.12 The size and _____ characteristics of a group of people ultimately depend upon the soil and climate of the area.

3.13 The Arunta obtain their food by a. _____ and b. _____ .

3.14 The Arunta _____ camp after the food supply in an area is used up.

3.15 Arunta social celebrations are held at a water hole during the _____ season.

3.16 In their wandering search for food, the Arunta carry few _____ .

Horticulturists. Horticulturists grow food crops. They can be thought of as farmers who do not fertilize or water their crops. They rely on the natural fertility of the soil and rain for good crops. When the fertility of the soil is **depleted**, usually in one or two years, they must relocate their fields. In times of drought, they must move or resort to hunting for food gathering. The Yąnomamö are horticulturists who live in the forested **watershed** of the Orinoco River in South America. They live in scattered villages, each averaging seventy to eighty people. The forest around each village is cleared for crops of plantains, bananas, maize, sweet potatoes, and manioc. Yąnomamö men also hunt monkeys, turkeys, wild pigs, armadillos, tapir, and alligators.

Horticulturists stay close to their crops to protect them from enemies and animals. When the soil in the village area is depleted or friction between people is leading to warfare, the Yąnomamö will move to a new location. The Yąnomamö live in a large circular community house. Each family has its own living area within the house. All of the vines, poles, and leaves for the house are found in the surrounding forest. The rain forest environment also contains stone for ax heads and wood for ax handles, bows, and arrows.

The Hopi of northern Arizona are horticulturists. They grow maize, beans, squash, and pumpkins. They live in permanent villages of stone apartments located on flat, tabletop mountains. The Hopi plant their crops in soil that is renewed each year through the addition of windblown top soil. They do not have to relocate their fields periodically. Hopi society is organized into **clans**. The clans provide for the political and religious functions of the villages. Ceremonies are associated with the agricultural cycle and the need for rain.

Fishing societies. Fishing communities differ from hunting communities in several ways. Fishing communities are not nomadic—their food supply does not migrate. Fishing communities can be quite large because fish are not easily depleted. **Durable** houses, large food reserves, and wealth distinguish fishing from hunting societies. The Haida are a fishing society located on the Pacific shores of British Colombia. They use nets and **wicker** baskets to catch salmon in the rivers. Herring are caught with dip nets, while hook and line are used for cod, halibut, and other deep water fish. Before the Europeans influenced the area, the Haida would hold great feasts, or *potlatches*. Great stores of wealth would be given away at these feasts. The Haida also acquired slaves by war and purchase. Several families would occupy a large plank house. They would have claim to a specific fishing territory.

Pastoralists. Pastoral societies depend on herds of domesticated animals for their food. Most pastoralists are nomadic. They move their herds from one grazing land to another when the seasons change. Animals domesticated by nomadic pastoralists include sheep, goats, cattle, horses, camels, and reindeer. The Nuer of the southern Sudan in Africa herd cattle. The cattle supply everything the Nuer need for daily life. Nuer diet consists mainly of milk and cheese. Cattle are only butchered for their meat when they are too old for milking or breeding. Cattle dung is used as a fuel for the homestead fire and the ashes provide a tooth-cleansing powder. The dung also serves as a plaster for the walls of their thatch-roofed houses. Cattle urine is used as a body pest repellent and hair oil. The land of the Nuer is relatively flat. During the dry season the Nuer gather together in small villages around water holes. When the summer rains come, the water hole areas become flooded and grass begins to grow too high. The villages break up and the cattle are herded to higher ground and better grazing. During this time the Nuer live in huts scattered around the countryside. Each family herd will then have enough grazing land.

Answer these questions.

3.17   The Yąnomamö obtain their food by a. _____
        and b. _____ .

3.18   Horticulturists live near their crops to give them _____ .

3.19   Because they do not fertilize the soil, horticulturists usually
        _____ their fields after a few years.

3.20   The a. _____ of northern Arizona do not move their fields
        because b. _____ topsoil renews them each year.

3.21   Some Hopi ceremonies are concerned with the need for _____ .

Write *true* or *false* in the blank.

3.22   _____   Fishing communities are not nomadic.

3.23   _____   The food supply of fishing communities is easily depleted.

3.24   _____   The Haida were very poor people.

3.25 _____ The Haida would hold great feasts called potlatches.

3.26 _____ Fishing societies have more durable houses than hunting societies.

Complete these activities.

3.27 Why are most pastoralists nomadic? Circle the correct answer.
a. They like to move
b. They must move their herds to new grazing land
c. Their herds will not stay in one place

3.28 Put a check beside the following items that the Nuer get from their cattle.
_____ food
_____ fuel
_____ grooming supplies
_____ wall plaster

3.29 Nuer gather together in small villages during the a. _____ season, but after the summer b. _____ come, they live c. _____ around the countryside.

SEEKING PROTECTION

People need protection from the elements of their environment and from those who would harm them. To obtain protection from their environments, people build shelters. The style, size, and construction of a shelter will depend on both the environment and culture of a society. Increased protection from enemies is usually accomplished through making an **alliance** with other people who will give help when it is needed.

Shelters. Shelters are usually made from local materials. They are usually designed to give the protection needed in a particular climate. They also will reflect the **lifestyle** of the builders. For example, in the winter the Eskimo hunt seal on the frozen Arctic Ocean. They require a durable structure. The shelter must give protection from the wind, and last the whole season. It must also be made of material that does not have to be carried long distances. To meet these requirements, the Eskimo developed the igloo, a hemispherical house made from blocks of hard snow.

Each igloo is built to house one hunter and his family. Several igloos are often clustered together, and connected with short tunnels. Although seal hunting requires

Eskimo Igloo

only one person, three or four men will usually hunt together. Their combined efforts should give greater success in providing food for their families.

Arunta brush shelter

Groups that occupy desert areas constantly move around in search of food. They need a disposable or portable house. Desert nomads can protect themselves from the sun and wind by building a brush shelter.

Brush shelters are made by pushing some sticks into the ground and piling bushes against them. When the food supply in an area is exhausted, the brush shelter can be abandoned. Hunting and gathering societies in desert environments are organized into small bands for effective hunting. Their shelter placement will reflect their loose social organization. Two or three family shelters will be settled together but far removed from any others. Those nomads who pasture animals in areas of sparse vegetation require a portable shelter. They must continually be moving around in search of food for their animals. The portable shelters are often made from the products of the herd. Tents are made from skins and from animal hair. The number of tents located in one place is related to the size of each family's herd and the amount of available vegetation.

In areas of heavy rainfall permanent structures are needed. Material that will not easily rot is used for shelters. The fishing communities along the North Pacific Coast of North America made large plank houses out of durable red cedar. Because their food supply did not shift location, fishing societies remained in the same location year after year. If a group had to shift its location, new shelters would be made. For easy repair, they were made from material that was readily replaced. Roofs of thatched leaves placed over a pole framework are common in rain forests of the world.

People need to remain near their food supplies. In general, those who depend on horticulture, agriculture, or fishing will have relatively permanent shelters. The people who follow migrating animals, herding them or hunting them, will use portable and disposable shelters.

- -

Answer these questions.

3.30   Why is an igloo an ideal shelter for seal hunters on the Arctic Ocean?

_____

_____

_____

3.31   Why is a brush shelter ideal for desert nomads?_____

_____

_____

_____

_____

Write the correct letter(s) on the blank. Two items may apply.

3.32   _____   relatively permanent shelters

3.33   _____   portable or disposable shelters

3.34   _____   cluster of few individuals shelters

3.35   _____   animal product shelters

a. hunting and gathering societies

b. fishing societies

c. horticultural societies

d. pastoral societies

Alliances. An individual is allied to the members of his family by birth. Family members normally provide help to individuals in times of growth and trouble. God's plan for creation establishes the family as the basic unit of man's life. The immediate family is to provide for an individual's upbringing. The extended family group provides assistance in times of trouble and need.

Most small societies are groups of kin who stand together against their foes. When one kin-group is not strong enough to protect itself, a related group can be called to help. The two sides in a quarrel will usually call enough kin to balance the dispute. An alliance for defense can be made with an unrelated group. Such an alliance is usually created by **intermar-**riage. Intermarriage establishes a tie of kinship between the two groups. Kin by marriage and kin by descent have an **obligation** for **mutual** support. These kin groups have a responsibility toward each other.

The Yąnomamö groups are noted for their fierceness and fighting. If one village loses several men in battle, it will usually seek an alliance with a stronger village. The alliance will be formed when females from the weakened village are married to men in the stronger village. The men in the stronger village are then obliged to give aid to the relatives of their new wives. However, the weaker village is also obligated to the stronger. When the men of the stronger village determine to raid some distant group, they can expect to receive assistance from their new wives' kin.

Complete these statements.

3.36   Most small societies are groups of _____ .

3.37   Alliances for support can be made with an unrelated group by

_____ .

3.38   An obligation for mutual support exists between two groups tied together by _____ .

3.39   In making an alliance, Yąnomamö women of the a. _____ .
        village are married to men of the b. _____ village.

3.40   In a Yąnomamö alliance the men of the stronger village expect the men of the weaker village to help them in their _____.

SEEKING PROSPERITY

People in every society believe in the existence of some form of supernatural power. They believe this power could be a personal spirit or a kind of force **inherent** in natural objects. That power or its influence is believed to add supernatural ability to a person or his property. People depend on that power to be successful in life. The ways in which people seek after that power are varied. The more common ways include visions, magic, and divination.

Visions. The Crow Indians of the Plains sought power through visions. They believed supernatural beings would appear to them in a vision and would give them the power they sought to be successful. The being in the vision would teach the person to sing a certain song or to wear something special on his head. These special signs indicated to the rest of the group that a person had a vision and now had extra ability or power. Visions for a Crow could come unsought or sought through a form of ordeal. A Crow might have a vision by fasting in the mountains, or by cutting off a finger. By treating himself so badly, the Crow was showing the supernatural beings his earnest desire for a vision. He expected his misery to get their attention and help.

Answer these questions.

3.41   Why do people seek after supernatural powers? _____

_____

3.42   How did the Crow Indians seek power for success? _____

_____

3.43   How could a Crow obtain a vision? _____

_____

_____

3.44   How would a Crow show he has had a vision? _____

_____

_____

Magic. In anthropology *magic* is defined as following a formula for doing things that are beyond one's personal powers. When an Indian places a fish in a hill to provide fertility to the soil, we call that *science*. The rotting fish provides chemicals to the soil to be used as **nutriments** by the corn. However, when a Zande from Africa puts the juice of one of his medicine plants in a patch of corn to provide fertility, we call that *magic*. Although the Zande has confidence in his procedure, the juice does not furnish chemicals the corn will need. To say that the Indian is scientific and the Zande is magical would be a mistake. The Indian is not relying on his knowledge of science when the fish is buried with the corn. Both the Zande and the Indian are relying on a supernatural force to grow a good crop.

However, only the Indian's method will affect the corn. We know that relying on methods of magic instead of living by God's laws in creation does not produce the desired results.

Another example of magic is seen in very old caves in Europe. The caves have pictures of wounded animals drawn on the walls. Anthropologists say these pictures are a magical attempt to achieve a successful hunt by first drawing the event. The picture is supposed to produce what it shows because of an unseen tie between the drawn hunt and the real hunt. If the animal is shown wounded in the picture, it will be wounded in the actual hunt. The belief that a magical connection exists between separate things in the world is still held by many people. For example, in some parts of Melanesia a man's battle wounds will be bandaged and treated with medicine. Depending on the nature of the wound, this treatment is sufficient. However, the arrow that wounded him also will be bandaged and treated with medicine. The arrow is treated to help the healing process and to ensure that the man recovers. This act is magic.

Cave painting

Answer these questions.

3.45 _____ is following a formula for doing things that are beyond one's personal power.

3.46 How does the Indian's method of helping corn to grow differ from the Zande's method?_____

_____

_____

_____

3.47 How is the Indian's method of helping corn to grow the same as the Zande's method?_____

_____

3.48 After some Melanesians bandage an arrow wound, they practice magic by also bandaging the _____ .

Divination. Any method for getting information about the future or knowledge about things otherwise hidden by reading life signs is *divination*. Divination is based on the assumption that all components of nature and life are connected together. Nothing is a matter of chance. Hidden information can be discovered either by omens or by oracles.

Omens are things that are seen and considered to be significant and meaningful. Omens are almost always related to events of nature. The widespread omen system of astrology uses the relationships of the stars and planets to gain information. These relationships are supposed to reveal a person's future. Eclipses, comets, meteors, and lightning are also considered by some people to be omens.

In many societies the behavior of animals is seen as a warning or a blessing. Animal behavior will influence special or large-scale community projects in some societies. The people of central Borneo will not start to build a house without a positive omen from the birds. Their houses could be up to four hundred yards long and take many days to complete. The people want some assurance that the project will be successful. Once the house is under construction, small boys are sent out to keep the birds away. If a negative omen were seen, the construction of the house would be stopped.

Oracles give "yes/no" information. They require a manipulation or experiment to get an answer. The Zande use several oracles, each to answer questions of differing importance. For simple problems, a Zande will cut two sticks of different kinds of wood. He will use the sticks to poke a hole in the side of a termite mound. When the swarming termites emerge, he will speak to them. He asks them his question and tells them to eat one stick if the answer is yes and eat the other if it is *no*. Then the sticks are placed in the hole and left there all night. The next day they are removed to see which stick the termites ate. The termite marks on them are "read" as either *yes* or *no*.

Zande rubbing board

For quick answers to everyday problems a Zande will use a rubbing board. The rubbing board is a small wooden platform with a flat top about the size of a man's hand. The platform has a matching piece of wood that is pushed back and forth on the platform top. Juice or soft pulp from a certain fruit is placed between the two pieces of wood. The properties of the wood and the juice produce a definite action. Either the upper piece of wood will continue to glide smoothly over the platform or it will quickly stick to it very tightly. When a Zande wants to know how to handle an everyday problem, he asks the rubbing board his question. He tells it to stick for a *yes* and slide for a *no*.

In matters of great importance, the Zande use an **alkaloid** poison called *benge*. It is fed to chickens and has the strange property of killing some chickens and leaving others unaffected. A Zande will address the benge and explain the whole problem which needs to be solved. The benge is told to kill the chicken if one answer is right or spare the chicken if the other answer is correct. The benge is then fed to the chicken. After several minutes, the chicken will either have a quick death or suffer no harm whatsoever. The decisions reached through a benge oracle have the force of law. They must be honored.

Write the correct letter in the blank.

3.49   Divination is any method for getting information about hidden things by
_____ .
a. asking someone   c. thinking real hard
b. reading signs   d. reading a book

3.50   The relationships of the stars and planets and other natural events are considered by some people to be _____ .
a. oracles   c. omens
b. magic   d. chance

3.51   Oracles require a manipulation or experiment and provide _____ information.
a. if/then   c. either/or
b. why/because   d. yes/no

3.52   For everyday problems requiring a quick answer the Zande use a
_____ .
a. rubbing board   c. termite
b. benge   d. chicken

3.53   The Zande oracle having the force of law depends on the action of a
_____ .
a. termite   c. fruit juice
b. judge   d. poison

Complete this activity.

3.54   Find the word *divination* in a Bible dictionary. Read the information and Bible verses listed. Write what the Word of God teaches about divination.

_____

_____

_____

_____

Teacher check _____

Initial   Date

Before you take this last Self Test, you may want to do one or more of these self checks.

1. _____ Read the objectives. See if you can do them.

2. _____ Restudy the material related to any objectives that you cannot do.

3. _____ Use the SQ3R study procedure to review the material:

   a. **S**can the sections.
   b. **Q**uestion yourself.
   c. **R**ead to answer your questions.
   d. **R**ecite the answers to yourself.
   e. **R**eview areas you did not understand.

4. _____ Review all vocabulary, activities, and Self Tests, writing a correct answer for every wrong answer.

SELF TEST 3

Match these items (each answer, 2 points).

3.01	_____ fieldwork	a.	sought visions through ordeal
3.02	_____ Negrid	b.	study people where they live
3.03	_____ Arunta	c.	produces homozygous population
3.04	_____ Yąnomamö	d.	descendants of Ham
3.05	_____ ethnologist	e.	use many oracles
3.06	_____ words	f.	hunters and gatherers
3.07	_____ Crow	g.	pastoralists
3.08	_____ archaeologist	h.	gain support through alliances
3.09	_____ Hopi	i.	fishing society
3.010	_____ phenotype	j.	studies contemporary societies
3.011	_____ anthropology	k.	the science of man
3.012	_____ Haida	l.	sounds with specific meanings
3.013	_____ Nuer	m.	physical characteristics
3.014	_____ Zande	n.	studies ancient societies
3.015	_____ intramarriage	o.	continue to plant same field

Write the correct letter in the blank (each answer, 2 points).

3.016 To anthropologists, human groups are like _____ .
   a. tools   c. cultures
   b. societies   d. laboratories

3.017 To see all seasonal activities, anthropologists should stay on the field at least _____ .
   a. one week   c. one month
   b. one year   d. one century

40

3.018 Anthropologists learn about the regularities in culture by using the _____.
   a. tape recorder   c. comparative method
   b. kinship chart   d. rites of passage

3.019 Man has value because he is made _____.
   a. out of dust   c. out of 206 bones
   b. by God   d. in God's image

3.020 Horticulturists live near their crops to give them _____.
   a. fertilizer   c. water
   b. protection   d. magic

3.021 To obtain food for their animals, most pastoralists are _____.
   a. nomadic   c. farmers
   b. wealthy   d. kin

3.022 Because they continually move about, hunters and gatherers have _____.
   a. no friends   c. few possessions
   b. sore feet   d. no shelters

3.023 The Indian who places a fish in the soil to rot and helps the corn grow is practicing _____.
   a. magic   c. divination
   b. science   d. religion

3.024 The Zande who puts plant juice in his corn patch to help it grow is practicing _____.
   a. magic   c. divination
   b. science   d. religion

3.025 When a Melanesian tries to heal a wound by bandaging the arrow that struck him, what is he practicing? _____
   a. magic   c. divination
   b. science   d. religion

3.026 Shelters are usually made from what? _____
   a. brick   c. cheap materials
   b. mud   d. local materials

3.027 The evaluation of culture from the native person's point of view is called _____.
   a. anthropology   c. method
   b. relativism   d. bias

Complete these statements (each answer, 3 points).

3.028 Culture is the ability of man to _____ his environment.

3.029 The scientific classification of man is _____.

3.030 Social cooperation is very difficult without a common _____.

3.031 Ties of kinship are formed through descent and _____.

3.032 _____ societies depend on herds of domesticated animals for their food.

3.033 To know the future of hidden things, people work acts of
_____ .

3.034 List three of the "rites of passage" Arnold van Gennep found that all societies celebrate.

a. _____

b. _____

c. _____

3.035 The elements necessary for a race to be formed are a(n) a. _____ , _____ , and a common b. _____ .

Write *true* **or** *false* **in the blank** (each answer, 1 point).

3.036 _____ Alleles control a phenotype.

3.037 _____ Races are people homozygous for many of the same genes.

3.038 _____ The Bible does not teach that races exist.

3.039 _____ The Bible does not teach that all men are the same.

3.040 _____ Fishing communities are usually nomadic.

3.041 _____ Joking, greetings, family, and music are cultural universals.

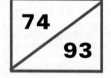

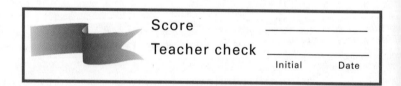

Score _____

Teacher check _____
　　　　　　　　　Initial　　　Date

Before taking the LIFEPAC Test, you may want to do one or more of these self checks.

1. _____ Read the objectives. See if you can do them.

2. _____ Restudy the material related to any objectives that you cannot do.

3. _____ Use the SQ3R study procedure to review the material.

4. _____ Review activities, Self Tests, and LIFEPAC vocabulary words.

5. _____ Restudy areas of weakness indicated by the last Self Test.